The Quiz

Written by Cathy Collins
Illustrated by Eric Mendez

Phonics Skills

Consonant Yy /y/		Consonant Qq /kw/	
yes	yak	quiz	quit

Jim will get a quiz.
Jim and Mom come in.
Jim and Mom sit.

Can Mom help Jim?
Yes, Mom can help him.
Jim sat. Mom sat.

"Jim, is a yak an ox?"
Jim sat. Jim said,
"A yak is not an ox."

"Jim, where is the big yak?"
Jim sat. Jim said,
"The big yak is on top."

"Jim, add six plus four."
Jim sat.
Six plus four is ten.

Jim will quit.

Jim will run fast.

Jim will get on the bus.

Jim got the quiz.
Can Jim pass?
Yes, Jim did!